The Moon

CHRISTINE TAYLOR-BUTLER

Children's Press®
An Imprint of Scholastic Inc.
New York Toronto London Auckland Sydney
Mexico City New Delhi Hong Kong
Danbury, Connecticut

Content Consultant
Bryan C. Dunne
Assistant Chair, Assistant Professor, Department of Astronomy
University of Illinois at Urbana–Champaign
Urbana, Illinois

Library of Congress Cataloging-in-Publication Data
Taylor-Butler, Christine.
The Moon / by Christine Taylor-Butler.
pages cm. — (A true book)
Includes bibliographical references and index.
ISBN 978-0-531-21154-0 (library binding) — ISBN 978-0-531-25360-1 (paperback)
1. Moon—Juvenile literature. I. Title.
QB582.T37 2014
523.3—dc23   2013029642

All rights reserved. Published in 2014 by Children's Press, an imprint of Scholastic Inc.
Printed in China 62
SCHOLASTIC, CHILDREN'S PRESS, A TRUE BOOK™, and associated logos are trademarks and/or
registered trademarks of Scholastic Inc.

1 2 3 4 5 6 7 8 9 10 R 23 22 21 20 19 18 17 16 15 14

**Front cover: Astronaut John Young saluting
the U.S. flag while jumping on the moon**

**Back cover: Astronaut Eugene Cernan
driving the lunar rover on the moon**

Find the Truth!

Everything you are about to read is true *except* for one of the sentences on this page.

Which one is **TRUE**?

T or F The moon's phases are the result of Earth's shadow falling on the moon.

T or F The same side of the moon always faces Earth.

Find the answers in this book.

3

Contents

1 Satellite in the Sky

How was the moon formed? 7

2 Craters and Highlands

What created the moon's large, dark regions? . . . 13

THE BIG TRUTH!

Tugging on Earth

What is the moon's connection
to ocean tides on Earth? 22

3 Light and Shadow

How can the moon block out the sun? . . . 25

In this view from the moon, Earth rises above the moon's horizon.

4 A Giant Leap Forward

When did humans first reach the moon? 31

5 Modern Lunar Missions

Will humans ever return to the moon? 39

True Statistics 44

Resources 45

Important Words 46

Index 47

About the Author 48

Twelve people have walked on the moon.

CHAPTER 1

Satellite in the Sky

The moon is the second-brightest object in the sky and Earth's only satellite. A satellite is an object such as a moon that **orbits** another, larger body in space. For thousands of years, the moon has fascinated humans. At night, the moon glows brightly in the sky because we see sunlight bouncing off its surface. In fact, the moon is so bright that you can still see it in the daytime.

← International law prevents nations from owning moons and planets.

The Moon's Origin

Where did the moon come from? There are many theories. Scientists' best theory today is that an object the size of Mars collided with Earth 4.5 billion years ago. The moon then formed from the molten, or melted, debris sent out by the impact. This explanation is supported by the fact that the moon's surface contains elements similar to Earth's crust.

Scientists are not sure how the moon formed, but since the 1970s, many have thought that it was the result of a giant collision.

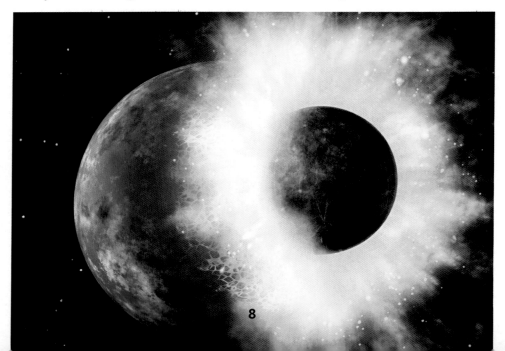

Earth is 24,901 miles (40,075 km) around, more than 3.5 times the distance around the moon.

Small Satellite

The moon is not very big compared to Earth. Fifty-one moons could fit inside our planet. The distance around the moon's middle is 6,783 miles (10,916 kilometers). If you cut the moon in half and measured from one side to the other, it would be less than 2,200 miles (3,540 km) across. That is about the distance from Los Angeles, California, to Chicago, Illinois. The moon's gravity is weaker than Earth's. On the moon, you feel only one-sixth of your weight on Earth.

The moon shines above Queensland in Australia.

The moon looks upside down in Australia, compared to how it looks in North America.

On Earth, we always see the same side of the moon. This is because the moon rotates on its **axis** at the same rate that it orbits Earth. In 27.3 Earth days, the moon completes one orbit and one rotation. As the moon rotates, it experiences its own day and night. Under the sun, surface temperatures on the moon are a scorching 253 degrees Fahrenheit (123 degrees Celsius). At night, it is −243°F (−153°C).

Like the **planets** in our solar system, the moon's orbit is not a perfect circle. Its orbit is an **ellipse**. Its farthest point from Earth is called the apogee. The moon is an average of about 250,000 miles (400,000 km) away at its apogee. The moon's closest point to Earth is called the perigee. This is an average of 225,000 miles (360,000 km) from Earth.

One year on Earth is about the same as 13 moon years.

The moon's orbit around Earth is not a perfect circle.

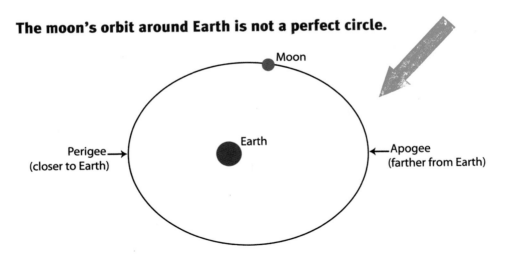

Moon

Earth

Perigee (closer to Earth)

Apogee (farther from Earth)

Astronaut Eugene Cernan salutes a U.S. flag during a mission to the moon in 1972.

CHAPTER 2

Craters and Highlands

The moon has no **geologic** activity today. Its **atmosphere** is essentially nonexistent. As a result, there is no wind erosion. Nothing inside or on the moon causes its surface to change. Evidence of the asteroids, comets, and meteoroids that have impacted the moon covers the lunar surface. Even footprints of visitors from Earth almost 50 years ago are still there.

There are six U.S. flags on the moon.

On the Surface

Like Earth, the moon has a crust. The crust is thinner on the side that faces the Earth and thicker on the side that faces away. Between 7 and 26 feet (2 to 8 meters) of powder called regolith cover the moon's surface. Meteoroids smashing into rocks over billions of years created this powdery blanket. The regolith is thickest in the moon's mountains and highlands.

Scientists recorded more than 300 meteoroid strikes on the lunar surface from 2005 to 2013.

Mare is the singular of *maria*. It means "sea" in Latin, though the moon's maria have no water.

Have you ever seen "the man in the moon"? This "face" is actually a pattern of dark regions on the moon's surface. These regions are deep impact craters called maria. They formed when large asteroids or comets hit the moon billions of years ago. At that time, the moon was geologically active. Molten rock from the moon's interior filled in the craters. The rock then cooled to become a dark mineral called basalt.

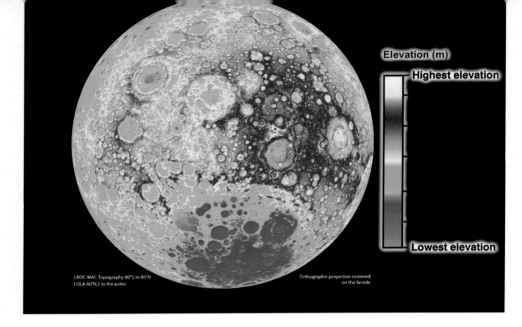

The large purple area at the bottom of the moon in this diagram marks the South Pole–Aitken basin.

The moon's largest crater is at its south pole. The South Pole–Aitken (SPA) basin is about 1,600 miles (2,575 km) wide. Geologists can estimate the age of a crater by its surface. Old craters generally have lots of other craters on top of them from more recent impacts. SPA is littered with younger craters. Scientists believe it to be the oldest impact basin on the moon. It is perhaps 3.9 billion years old.

The lighter areas on the moon are the highlands and mountains. They were formed early in the moon's history. Billions of years ago, the moon was largely hot, molten rock. A more lightweight mineral called feldspar floated in this magma. This formed the highlands and mountains that we see on the moon today. They are the oldest part of the moon's crust. They are covered with rocks that flew out of the moon's many craters.

The moon's highlands appear as lighter areas to the right of the maria in this photo. The area is dotted with craters.

Highlands

Maria

17

Below the Surface

Underneath the moon's crust is the **mantle**. The mantle is a cool, dense layer of rock. This is the moon's thickest layer. Beneath the mantle is a partially melted layer of rock. Beneath that is the core. The lunar core is similar to Earth's core, but much smaller. It is about 410 miles (660 km) across. The core is rich in iron and has two parts: the liquid outer core and the solid inner core.

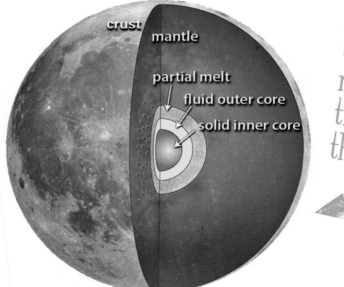

crust
mantle
partial melt
fluid outer core
solid inner core

A quake zone beneath the moon's mantle creates gentle tremors that vibrate the moon like a bell.

Part of Earth is visible in the moon's sky in this photo taken from the moon. White clouds cover Earth. However, with little atmosphere, the moon's dark sky is always cloudless.

Atmosphere? What Atmosphere?

Unlike Earth, the moon does not have a thick layer of gases to protect its surface. Spacecraft have proven that the moon does have an atmosphere, but it is incredibly thin. It is mostly made of sodium and potassium. Studies have also found traces of helium, argon, neon, ammonia, methane, and carbon dioxide on the moon.

When astronauts visited the moon in the 1960s and 1970s, they wore suits that protected them from extreme temperatures and provided plenty of oxygen.

The **density** of the moon's atmosphere is much lower than that of Earth's atmosphere. A less dense atmosphere means a lot less air. You cannot breathe without a special suit on the moon. On Earth, air molecules are so close together they bounce off each other. There is much more space between air molecules on the moon. They move freely, carried by charged particles from the sun.

The Supermoon

The moon reaches the perigee about once every month. If the moon is full when it reaches the perigee, it is called a perigee moon. Some people call it a supermoon. This moon appears to be 13 percent larger and 30 percent brighter than the moon on other days. Ocean tides are also slightly larger because the moon is closer to Earth.

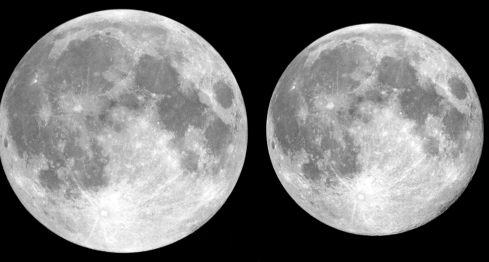

Perigee moon

Apogee moon

Tugging on Earth

Few people think about the moon when they watch an ocean tide roll in. But, in fact, the moon causes tides! Earth has two high tides and two low tides each lunar day. A lunar day is the time between one moonrise and the next moonrise. A lunar day is 24 hours and 50 minutes long.

The moon's gravity pulls Earth's water toward it. The water rises, or bulges toward the moon. This creates one high tide.

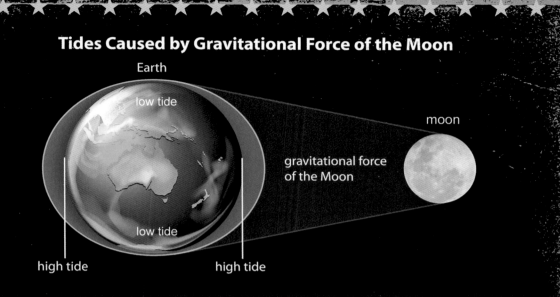

Tides Caused by Gravitational Force of the Moon

Earth

low tide

moon

gravitational force
of the Moon

low tide

high tide

high tide

Another high tide is on the side of Earth facing away from the moon. The moon's gravity tugs on Earth. This pulls Earth very slightly toward the moon. The water on the far side of Earth is left behind. As a result, it appears to bulge out toward space.

In between the two bulges, the lower levels of water create low tides. As Earth rotates, the tidal bulges stay aligned with the moon, and a location moves from high tide to low tide to high tide, and so on.

CHAPTER 3

Light and Shadow

The moon's appearance is constantly changing. Sometimes it shines as a full, bright circle in the night sky. At other times, parts of the moon seem to disappear, only to reappear later. People on Earth have watched these **phases** for thousands of years. The phases have inspired myths and helped people measure time. But what actually causes the changes in the moon's appearance?

The moon's gravitational pull helps keep Earth's rotation stable.

First quarter

Full

New

Changeable Moon

The moon shines by reflecting light from the sun. As the moon orbits Earth, the amount of lit side that faces Earth changes. As a result, the amount of the moon we can see from Earth changes. One full cycle takes about 29.5 Earth days. The moon has four primary phases: new, first quarter, full, and third quarter.

Third quarter

New

When the moon appears more than half lit, it is a gibbous moon. When it appears less than half lit, it is a crescent moon.

When the dark side of the moon faces Earth, it is a new moon. Then the moon **waxes**. When it appears half lit, the moon is at first quarter. When fully lit, it is a full moon. Then the moon **wanes**. Its daylight side turns away from Earth. When a waning moon appears half lit, it is in its third quarter.

The moon appears red only while Earth's shadow covers it completely.

A Blood-Red Moon

A lunar **eclipse** occurs only when the sun, moon, and Earth are lined up during a full moon. Earth blocks the sun, and the moon turns dark. In a partial lunar eclipse, Earth's shadow passes over part of the moon. In a total lunar eclipse, Earth blocks the sun completely. But at the edge of Earth, the planet's atmosphere bends red light from the sun into the shadow. This gives the moon an eerie, reddish glow.

Eclipsing the Sun

The sun is about 400 times the moon's size. However, the moon is about 400 times closer to Earth than the sun is. This makes the two objects appear close to the same size in Earth's sky. Sometimes a new moon can block part of the sun for viewers on Earth in a solar eclipse. In a more rare total solar eclipse, the moon completely blocks the sun. Then the sun's outer atmosphere, the corona, becomes temporarily visible.

Each total solar eclipse can be seen from only part of Earth.

This diagram shows how the sun, moon, and Earth are lined up to create a solar eclipse.

CHAPTER 4

A Giant Leap Forward

Since ancient times, people have told stories to explain the moon. Ancient Inuits called the moon Igaluk. Igaluk was a god who controlled the weather and sea animals. The Greeks named the moon after the goddess Selene. According to Greek myth, Selene drove her silver chariot, the moon, across the sky. Romans connected the moon to the goddess Diana.

In ancient Mesopotamia, the moon god was associated with the bull, because the crescent moon resembled bull horns.

Early Observations

Early astronomers in China and the Middle East were able to predict eclipses. In ancient Greece, mathematician Hipparchus estimated the moon's distance from Earth. In the 17th century, Italian astronomer Galileo Galilei improved on early telescopes. This allowed him to see mountains and valleys on the moon's surface. German astronomer Johannes Kepler named the moon's lighter areas terrae and darker spots maria. Modern astronomers still use Kepler's names for surface features.

Johannes Kepler was the first person to explain that the moon causes ocean tides on Earth.

Sputnik was launched on October 4, 1957, and orbited Earth for 21 days.

Reaching Space

Almost 350 years later, the Soviet Union built Earth's first human-made satellite. They called the satellite *Sputnik*. The spacecraft's mission was to study Earth from space. At first, the design was too complicated. The Soviets simplified their project and launched *Sputnik* in October 1957. The United States was still struggling with tests of its satellite *Vanguard* when *Sputnik*'s launch was announced. The United States wanted to keep up with the Soviets. The race to space was on!

Luna 2's inventors also called it the Second Cosmic Rocket.

To the Moon

The Soviet Union launched two spacecraft to the moon in 1959. They were named _Luna 1_ and _Luna 2_. The first missed its target and orbited the sun instead. _Luna 2_ hit the moon 33.5 hours after it was launched. It was the first spacecraft to reach the moon's surface.

In April 1961, Soviet astronaut Yuri Gagarin became the first person to travel into space. One month later, U.S. president John Kennedy pledged millions of dollars to help land an American on the moon. The National Aeronautics and Space Administration (NASA) then created its largest scientific mission: Project Apollo. NASA launched lunar orbiters between 1966 and 1967 to map the moon's surface. This information was used to develop the first manned spacecraft.

Yuri Gagarin's flight lasted 108 minutes.

On July 20, 1969, the *Apollo 11* spacecraft landed on the moon. Astronauts Neil Armstrong and Edwin "Buzz" Aldrin became the first men to walk on the moon. They planted an American flag there. When they returned to Earth, the astronauts were quarantined, or kept separate from the public, for three weeks. During this time, scientists conducted tests to prove the astronauts carried no germs from the moon.

Buzz Aldrin sets up an experiment on the moon.

Moon samples proved that the moon's crust is 4.4 billion years old.

36

Apollo astronauts used a spacecraft called a Lunar Module, or LM, to land on the moon.

By 1972, five more Apollo spacecraft and 10 more astronauts successfully landed on the moon. Astronauts collected a total of 842 pounds (382 kilograms) of rocks for scientists to study on Earth. A total of 20 missions were planned. However, government funding slowed. The remaining missions were canceled. In 2004, President George W. Bush pledged to return to the moon by 2020. But the program was later deemed too expensive. It was canceled in 2010.

CHAPTER 5

Modern Lunar Missions

Since the Apollo missions ended, no people have traveled to the moon. But that does not mean scientists are not exploring the lunar landscape in other ways. Space missions are being planned all over the world in the hope that we might go back someday. Now it is not just governments planning the trips, but companies as well.

← New designs for lunar vehicles have been tested in Hawaii.

Lunar Reconnaissance Orbiter (LRO)

LRO's mission is to create high-definition maps of the moon's surface. LRO was launched on June 18, 2009. It arrived at the moon five days later and entered into orbit around it. One exciting discovery was temperature readings in those dark craters. They never receive sunlight and average −397°F (−238°C).

Timeline of Moon Exploration

1969

Neil Armstrong and Buzz Aldrin become the first people to walk on the moon.

LCROSS

LCROSS is a shortened version of a much longer name: Lunar CRater Observation and Sensing Satellite. It was launched in 2009 with LRO. It was designed to find out whether the moon had water ice. In October 2009, LCROSS sent a piece of rocket plummeting into the moon's surface. When the object hit, it sent up a cloud of debris. LCROSS tested the debris and found water ice crystals!

2009
LCROSS discovers ice crystals near the moon's south pole.

2013
The LADEE satellite is launched.

1972
The final *Apollo* mission is completed.

The Lunar Atmosphere and Dust Environment Explorer (LADEE)

Apollo astronauts saw the moon's horizon glow just before sunrise. Now NASA scientists want to know why. Launched in 2013, LADEE is designed to study light in the moon's atmosphere and collect moondust. Information from LADEE and other spacecraft will help determine where future astronauts might visit on the moon. It will also help scientists plan for longer stays there. Such plans will take many years to complete. Perhaps you could be the next person on the moon!

LADEE traveled for 30 days before entering orbit around the moon.

Moon Base

Astronauts currently live on the International Space Station (ISS). Why don't they live on the moon? Engineering companies are working out how to make this possible. They will start by testing a scaled-down version of a lunar base. Inflatable test labs will also be sent to ISS in 2015. Eventually, engineers hope to land on the moon's surface and construct a full-scale base there.

Speed at which the moon travels around Earth: 2,287 mph (3,680 kph)

First person on the moon: Neil Armstrong, 1969

Number of people who have walked on the moon: 12

Last time a person landed on the moon: 1972

Depth of the deepest crater on the moon: 15,000 ft. (4,572 m)

Height of the highest mountain on the moon: 16,000 ft. (4,877 m)

Number of clouds on the moon: Zero

Number of active volcanoes on the moon: Zero

Did you find the truth?

(F) The moon's phases are the result of Earth's shadow falling on the moon.

(T) The same side of the moon always faces Earth.

Resources

Books

Aguilar, David A. *13 Planets: The Latest View of the Solar System*. Washington, DC: National Geographic, 2011.

Carson, Mary Kay. *Far-Out Guide to the Moon*. Berkeley Heights, NJ: Bailey Books, 2011.

Jemison, Mae, and Dana Meachen Rau. *Journey Through Our Solar System*. New York: Children's Press, 2013.

Visit this Scholastic Web site for more information on the moon:
★ www.factsfornow.scholastic.com
Enter the keywords **The Moon**

Important Words

atmosphere (AT-muhs-feer) — the mixture of gases that surrounds a planet

axis (AK-sis) — an imaginary line through the middle of an object, around which that object spins

density (DEN-suh-tee) — the amount of matter in an object

eclipse (i-KLIPS) — a time when Earth comes between the sun and the moon, or the moon comes between the sun and Earth, and blocks all or part of the sun's light

ellipse (i-LIPS) — a flat oval shape

geologic (jee-uh-LAH-jik) — having to do with a planet's physical structure

mantle (MAN-tuhl) — the part of Earth between the crust and the core

orbits (OR-bits) — travels in a path around something, especially a planet or the sun

phases (FAYZ-iz) — stages of the moon's change in shape as it appears from Earth

planets (PLAN-its) —large bodies orbiting a star

wanes (WAYNZ) — appears to become less or smaller in size

waxes (WAKS-iz) — appears to grow

Index

Page numbers in **bold** indicate illustrations

Aldrin, Edwin "Buzz," **36**, **40**
apogee, 11, **21**
Apollo missions, 35–**37**, **41**, 42
Armstrong, Neil, 36, 40
asteroids, 13, 15
astronauts, **12**, **20**, **35**, **36**, **37**, **40**, 42, 43
atmosphere, 13, **19**–20, 42
axis, 10, 26

brightness, 7, 21

comets, 13, 15
core, **18**
craters, 13, 15, **16**, **17**, 40
crescent moon, 27, 31
crust, 14, 17, 36

days, 10, 22
distance, 11, 32

Earth, **8**, **9**, **10**, **11**, **19**, 20, **22**–**23**, 25, 26, **28**, **29**, 33
eclipses, **28**, **29**, 32
erosion, 13

first quarter moon, **26**, 27
flags, **12**, 13, 36
full moon, **26**

geologic activity, 13, 15
gibbous moon, 27
gravity, 9, **23**

highlands, 14, **17**

lunar bases, **43**
Lunar Module (LM), **36**, **37**

lunar vehicles, **38**

mantle, **18**
maria, **15**, **17**, 32
meteoroids, 13, **14**
mountains, 14, 17, 32

new moon, **26**, **27**, 29

orbit, 7, **8**, 10, **11**, **33**, 35, 40, **42**
origin, **8**

perigee, 11, **21**
phases, 25, **26**–**27**

quake zone, 18

regolith, 14
rotation, 10, 23, 26

size, **9**, 29
solar eclipses, **29**
South Pole–Aitken (SPA) basin, **16**, 41
sun, 7, 10, 20, 26, 28, **29**, 34, 40
supermoon, 21

temperatures, 10, 20, 40
third quarter moon, **27**
tides, 21, **22**–**23**, 32
timeline, **40**–**41**

waning moon, 27
water, **15**, **19**, 23, 41
waxing moon, 27

years, 11

About the Author

Christine Taylor-Butler is the author of more than 65 books for children including the True Book series on American History/Government, Health and the Human Body, and Science Experiments. A graduate of the Massachusetts Institute of Technology, Taylor-Butler holds degrees in both civil engineering and art and design. She lives in Kansas City, Missouri.